SPELLING FOR

MINECRAFTERS

Grade 1

Illustrated by Amanda Brack

Sky Pony Press
New York

Sky Pony Press books may be purchased in bulk at special discounts for sales promotion, corporate gifts, fund-raising, or educational purposes. Special editions can also be created to specifications. For details, contact the Special Sales Department, Sky Pony Press, 307 West 36th Street, 11th Floor, New York, NY 10018 or info@skyhorsepublishing.com.

Sky Pony® is a registered trademark of Skyhorse Publishing, Inc.®, a Delaware corporation.

Visit our website at www.skyponypress.com.

Authors, books, and more at SkyPonyPressBlog.com.

10 9 8 7 6 5 4 3 2

Library of Congress Cataloging-in-Publication Data is available on file.

Cover design by Brian Peterson

Cover illustration by Bill Greenhead

Book design by Kevin Baier

Print ISBN: 978-1-5107-3762-4

Printed in China

A NOTE TO PARENTS

When you want to reinforce classroom skills at home, it's crucial to have kid-friendly learning materials. This *Spelling for Minecrafters* workbook transforms spelling practice into an irresistible adventure, complete with diamond swords, zombies, skeletons, and creepers. That means less arguing over homework and more fun overall.

Spelling for Minecrafters is also fully aligned with National Common Core Standards for 1st-grade spelling. What does that mean, exactly? All of the spelling skills taught in this book correspond to what your child is expected to learn in school. This eliminates confusion and builds confidence for greater homework-time success!

Whether it's the joy of seeing their favorite game characters on every page or the thrill of spelling with Steve and Alex, there is something in this workbook to entice even the most reluctant student.

Happy adventuring!

MISSING LETTER

What vowel is missing from the words below? Write it on the line.

1. c a t    CAT

2. h u g    hug

3. p i g    pig

4. b a t    bat

5. e gg    egg

BUILDING WORDS

Spell the words from the word box in the empty blocks below.
Use the shape of the blocks to help you.

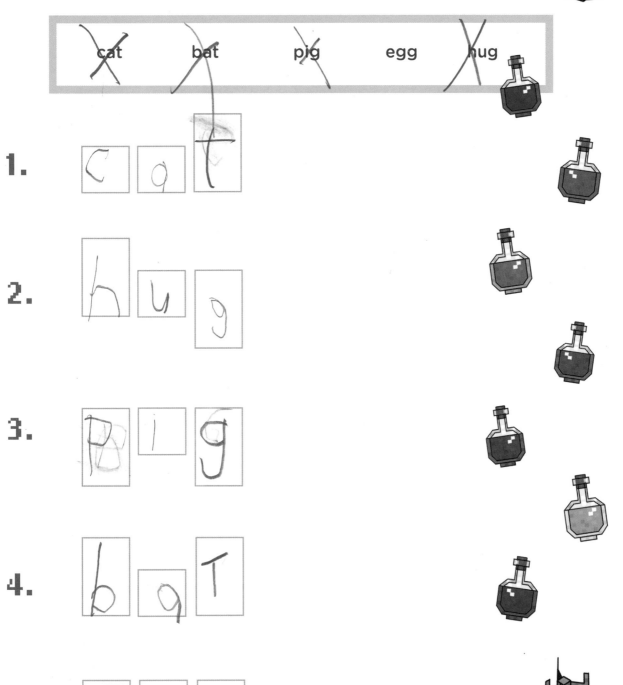

~~cat~~   ~~bat~~   ~~pig~~   egg   ~~hug~~

1. C a t

2. h u g

3. P i g

4. b a T

5. e g g

SIGHT WORD FILL-IN

Use the box of sight words to finish the sentences below.

and	over	~~her~~	~~how~~	~~walk~~	~~some~~

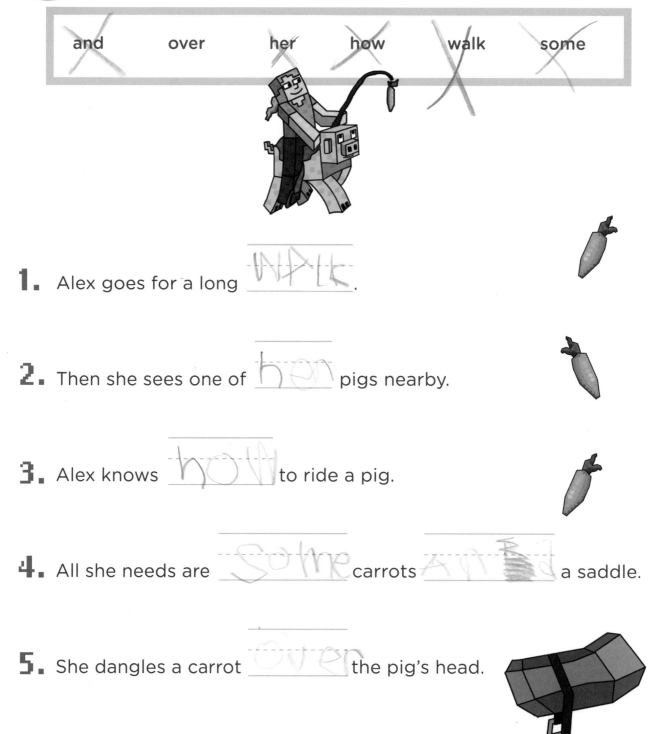

1. Alex goes for a long _WALK_.

2. Then she sees one of _her_ pigs nearby.

3. Alex knows _how_ to ride a pig.

4. All she needs are _some_ carrots _and_ a saddle.

5. She dangles a carrot _over_ the pig's head.

SIGHT WORD SCRAMBLE

Unscramble the sight words below. Write them correctly on the line. Use the word box on page 4 for help.

1. vore _____

2. woh _____

3. erh _____

4. dan _____

5. esom _____

6. kwla _____

SIGHT WORD WRITING CHALLENGE

Practice spelling the sight words below. Copy each word on the space provided. Check your work.

1. over   Oven

2. her   her

3. walk   walk

4. how   how

5. some   some

6. and   And

BEGINNING SOUNDS

Say the names of the pictures below. They have the same beginning sound! Circle the letter that has the matching beginning sound.

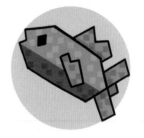

1.     b   p

2.    d   g

3.    c   r

4.   m   c

5.    t   f

PUNCTUATION POWER

Every sentence should have a capital letter in the beginning and punctuation (a period, question mark, or exclamation point) at the end.

These sentences are missing something. Write them correctly on the line below.

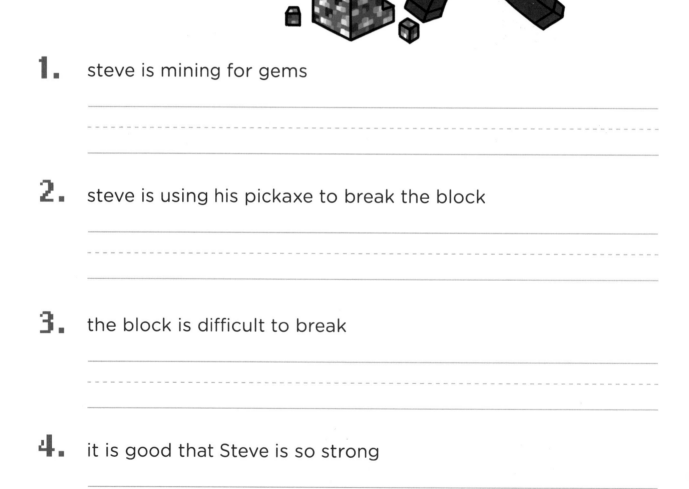

1. steve is mining for gems

_____

_____

2. steve is using his pickaxe to break the block

_____

_____

3. the block is difficult to break

_____

_____

4. it is good that Steve is so strong

_____

_____

MISSING LETTER

What vowel is missing from the words below? Write it on the line.

1. w _ b ....

2. s _ n ....

3. p _ n ....

4. r _ n ....

5. l _ g ....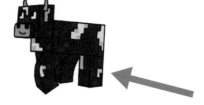

BUILDING WORDS

Spell the words from the word box in the empty blocks below.
Use the shape of the blocks to help you.

pen	web	sun	leg	run

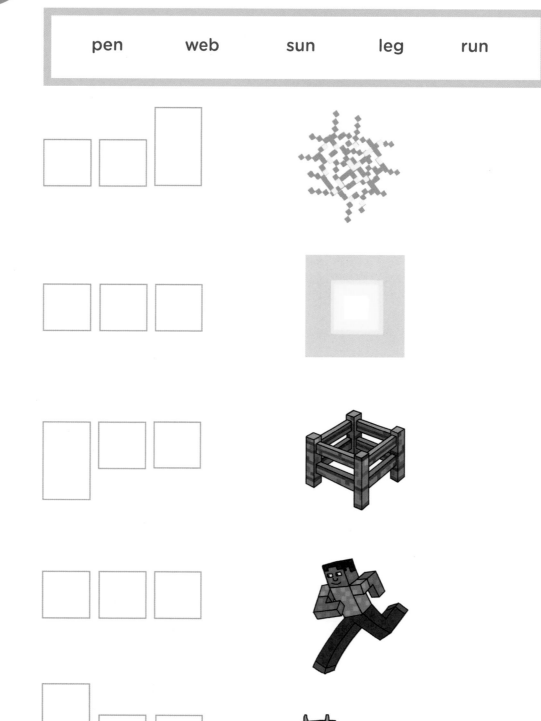

1.

2.

3.

4.

5.

SIGHT WORD FILL-IN

Use the box of sight words to finish the sentences below. If the word comes at the beginning of a sentence, be sure to use a capital letter.

all	both	that	go	use

1. _____ of these mooshrooms are happy.

2. Watch out for _____ creeper!

3. A zombie just ran off with _____ my loot!

4. You can _____ a pickaxe to break a block.

5. You need a portal to _____ to the Nether.

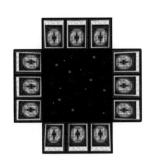

SIGHT WORD SCRAMBLE

Unscramble the sight words below. Write them correctly on the line. Use the word box on page 11 for help.

1. seu _____

2. otbh _____

3. lal _____

4. hatt _____

5. og _____

SIGHT WORD WRITING CHALLENGE

Practice spelling the sight words below. Copy each word on the space provided. Check your work.

1. all

2. both

3. that

4. go

5. use

SLIME'S RHYME CHALLENGE

Write a word that rhymes. Use the picture for help.

1. sun _____

2. leg _____

3. pen _____

4. up _____

Write a sentence about Minecraft using a pair of rhyming words.

_____

_____

_____

WORD CRAFTING

Steve wants to craft as many words as possible and needs your help. Make words with the letters shown and write them below.

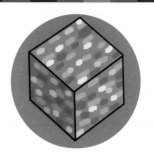

c n p

a e

t o

u f l

1. _____

2. _____

3. _____

4. _____

5. _____

6. _____

7. _____

8. _____

MISSING LETTER

What vowel is missing from each word below? Write it on the line.

1. d _ g ----------------------------

2. s _ x ----------------------------

3. b _ g ----------------------------

4. m _ bs ----------------------------

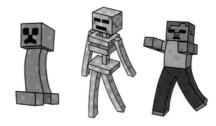

5. h _ p ----------------------------

BUILDING WORDS

Spell the words from the word box in the empty blocks below. Use the shape of the blocks to help you. Hint: Three of the words have the same shape blocks.

| dog | six | hop | big | mobs |

1.

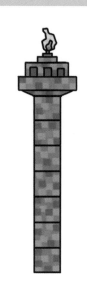

2.

3.

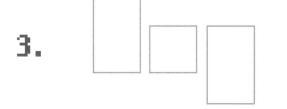

4.

5.

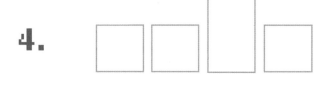

SIGHT WORD FILL-IN

Use the box of sight words to finish the sentences below.

| boy | from | look | play | will |

1. Steve is a brave _____.

2. I want to _____ Minecraft all day.

3. Don't _____ at an Enderman! It will attack.

4. The Enderman teleports _____ one place to another.

5. A ghast _____ shoot fireballs at you.

SIGHT WORD WRITING CHALLENGE

Practice spelling the sight words below. Copy each word on the space provided. Check your work.

1. boy

2. from

3. look

4. play

5. will

FIND AND FIX

Look for one spelling mistake in each sentence below. Cross out the misspelled word and write it correctly on the line.

1. The wolf pup wants to playe with Steve.

---

2. You wile love battling the Ender Dragon.

---

3. When it's dark, looke out for zombies.

---

4. Players can get emeralds form villagers.

---

5. Video games are fun for girls and boyz.

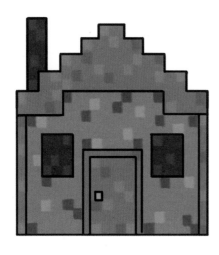

ENDING SOUNDS

Say the names of the pictures below. They have the same ending sound!

Circle the letter that has the matching ending sound.

1.   l   w

2.    m   n

3.   c   d

4.   t   r

5.   p   t

MISSING LETTER LONG VOWEL SOUNDS

The evoker stole the long vowel sounds from the words below. Rewrite the words with the missing vowels.

1. bl _ ze

2. b _ ne

3. c _ ve

4. wr _ te

All the words above have a silent "e" at the end that makes the vowel long. **Circle the silent "e" in the words above.**

What happens when you **add a silent "e" to the word below?** *Write the new word.*

5.

 →

cub

SIGHT WORD SCRAMBLE

Unscramble the vowel-consonant-e words below. Use the previous page to help you.

1. zlbae _____

2. nebo _____

3. rewit _____

4. evac _____

Answer the clues to write more vowel-consonant-e words below:

5. How many items does this player have?

_____

6. What do you see at the end of this torch?

_____

SIGHT WORD FILL-IN

Use the box of sight words to finish the sentences below.

the	she	it	has	are

1. The clock tells us when _____ will get dark.

2. The hungry cows _____ eating the hay.

3. I put my weapons in _____ chest.

4. The ghast _____ lots of legs and flies in the air.

5. Alex uses a sword when _____ battles the Wither.

BUILDING WORDS

Write the words from the word box in the empty blocks below. Use the shape of the blocks to help you. Hint: Two words have blocks that are the same shape.

| the | she | it | has | are |

1.

2.

3.

4.

5.

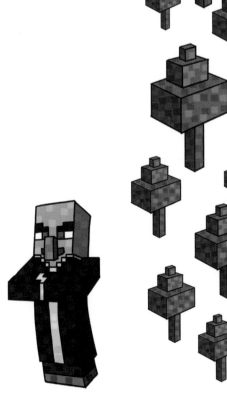

SIGHT WORD WRITING CHALLENGE

Practice spelling the sight words below. Copy each word on the space provided. Check your work.

1. the _____

2. she _____

3. it _____

4. has _____

5. are _____

FIND AND FIX

Look for a spelling mistake in each sentence below. Cross out the misspelled word and write the word correctly on the line.

1. Alex knows shi will win the battle.

_____

2. A map helps you find thu way home. _____

3. A Wither hass three heads.

_____

4. You should only eat beef if itt is cooked. _____

5. Villagers ar afraid of creepers, too!

_____

BEGINNING SOUND MATCH-UP

Draw a line from the word to the matching picture. Underline the consonant pair (ch, th, or sh) at the beginning of each word.

1. shulker

2. chest

3. thistle

4. think

5. chicken

6. shears

ENDING SOUND MATCH-UP

Draw a line from the word to the matching picture.
Underline the consonant pair (ch, sh, or th) at the end of
each word.

1. torch

2. witch

3. fish

4. hatch

5. push

6. mouth

LONG AND SHORT VOWELS

Fill in the missing vowel to complete the word. Circle long or short to describe the sound the vowel makes.

1. 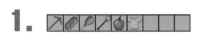   __nventory   **LONG**   **SHORT**

2.   t__me   **LONG**   **SHORT**

3.   __nk sac   **LONG**   **SHORT**

4.   sl__me   **LONG**   **SHORT**

5.   v__llager   **LONG**   **SHORT**

LONG AND SHORT VOWELS

Fill in the missing vowel to complete the word. Circle long *or* short *to describe the sound the vowel makes.*

1.  __nderman   **LONG**   **SHORT**

2. tr__ __   **LONG**   **SHORT**

3. sh__ __p   **LONG**   **SHORT**

4.  sk__l__ton   **LONG**   **SHORT**

5. b__ __f   **LONG**   **SHORT**

LONG AND SHORT VOWELS

Fill in the missing vowel to complete the word. Circle long or short to describe the sound the vowel makes.

1. arr__w   **LONG**   **SHORT**

2. z__mbie   **LONG**   **SHORT**

3. bl__ck   **LONG**   **SHORT**

4. gl__wstone   **LONG**   **SHORT**

5. p__tion   **LONG**   **SHORT**

LONG AND SHORT VOWELS

Fill in the missing vowel to complete the word. Circle long *or* short *to describe the sound the vowel makes.*

1. __xe   **LONG   SHORT**

2.  att__ck   **LONG   SHORT**

3. c__ke   **LONG   SHORT**

4.  h__t   **LONG   SHORT**

5. gh__st   **LONG   SHORT**

LONG AND SHORT VOWELS

Fill in the missing vowel to complete the word. Circle long or short to describe the sound the vowel makes.

1.   p__fferfish   **LONG**   **SHORT**

2.   c__be   **LONG**   **SHORT**

3.   bl__e   **LONG**   **SHORT**

4.    h__sk   **LONG**   **SHORT**

5.   dr__mstick   **LONG**   **SHORT**

SIGHT WORD FILL-IN

Use the box of sight words to finish the sentences below.

can	you	we	said	do

1. If you have a portal, you _____ go to the Nether.

2. My friend _____ he would play video games with me.

3. _____ fight the Ender dragon with our enchanted weapons.

4. The first thing you should _____ is craft a bed out of wood.

5. _____ need food to fill your hunger bar.

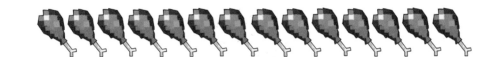

SIGHT WORD SCRAMBLE

Unscramble the sight words below. Write them correctly on the line. Use the word box on page 35 for help.

1. od _____

2. dias _____

3. nca _____

4. oyu _____

5. ew _____

SIGHT WORD WRITING CHALLENGE

Practice spelling the sight words below. Copy each word on the space provided. Check your work.

1. can

2. you

3. we

4. said

5. do

RHYME TIME

Write the word that rhymes with the word in bold.

| ladder | table | sword | slow | potion |

1. When I'm feeling very **bored**, I like to craft a

diamond _____ .

2. My hunger bar is getting **low**, so I am moving

extra _____ .

3. If I mine things, then I'm **able** to make things on

a crafting _____ .

4. When I'm swimming in the **ocean**, I brew myself

a breathing _____ .

5. Go ahead and climb; it doesn't **matter**! Mobs will

chase you up a _____ .

COUNT THE SYLLABLES

Read the words and count the number of syllables. Write the number on the line.

How many syllables?

1. creeper

_____

2. zombie

_____

3. skeleton

_____

4.  ghast

_____

5. Enderman

_____

WORD CRAFTING

Alex opened an enchanted chest and found these letters.
Help her craft as many words as you can. Write them below.

m   n   s

a   d

                         e

o   r

   b   i

1. _____

2. _____

3. _____

4. _____

5. _____

6. _____

7. _____

8. _____

PUNCTUATION POWER

Every sentence should have a capital letter in the beginning and punctuation (a period, question mark, or exclamation point) at the end.

These sentences are missing something. Write them correctly on the line below.

1. there are many zombies

_____

2. zombie pigmen live in the Nether

_____

3. zombies attack villagers

_____

4. zombies burn in the daylight

_____

5. they come out at night

_____

CREEPER'S CAPITAL LETTER QUEST

Creeper knows that names begin with a capital letter. Rewrite the sentences below and add capital letters where they are needed.

1. When alex saw the ocelot, she ran over to it.

2. steve gave alex some fish so she could tame it.

3. The ocelot ate alex's fish and turned into a cat.

4. alex named her pet cat savannah.

5. savannah scared away all the creepers.

FIND AND FIX

Look for a spelling mistake in each sentence below. Cross out the misspelled word and write the word correctly on the line.

1. You can doo lots of things with enchanted weapons.

   _____

2. My brother sed you can get more items with enchanted weapons.

   _____

3. Enchanted swords kan set anything on fire.

   _____

4. One day, wee enchanted our pickaxes.

   _____

5. Yew won't believe how much loot we got!

   _____

VOWEL TEAMS

The vowel teams below make the long e sound. Write the missing letter on the line.

1.

w__eat

_____

2.

me__t

_____

3.

g__een

_____

4.

fee__

_____

5.

cre__per

_____

6.

__ree

_____

7. What vowel teams do you see in the words above?

_____   _____

_____   _____

VOWEL TEAMS

Write the missing letter on the line.

1.

mush__oom

_____

2.

__eetroot

_____

3.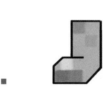

moo__

_____

4.

mo__d

_____

5.

__oot

_____

6.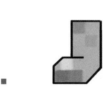

t__ol

_____

7. What vowel teams do you see in the words above?

_____

_____

SLIME'S RHYME CHALLENGE

Read each pair of words. If they rhyme, check the box.

It's a rhyme!

1. Grass   Glass   ☐

2. Enderman   Endermite   ☐

3. Slime   Time   ☐

4. Craft   Blast   ☐

5. Teeth   Wheat   ☐

6. Armor   Farmer   ☐

BEGINNING BLENDS

Say the word out loud. Circle the correct beginning blend.

1.  _____agon   **dr**   **br**   **dv**

2. _____eve   **Sl**   **St**   **Sn**

3. _____aze   **br**   **bt**   **bl**

4. _____ider   **sp**   **sl**   **sc**

5. _____ow golem **st**   **sc**   **sn**

6. _____uid   **st**   **sq**   **sl**

ENDING BLENDS

Say the word out loud. Circle the correct ending blend.

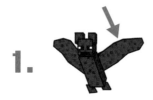

1. wi_____   ng   nd   nt

2. firewo_____   rt   rd   rk

3. swo_____   rt   rd   rn

4. gha_____   sl   sr   st

5. shie_____   ld   lm   lt

6.  enchanted che_____   sk   st   sp

COUNT THE SYLLABLES

Read the words and count the number of syllables.
Write the number on the line.

How many syllables?

1. iron golem _____

2. shulker _____

3. silverfish _____

4. guardian _____

5.  squid _____

49

FIND THE SILENT LETTER

Which letter in the words below is silent? Circle the letter and write it on the space provided.

1. sword _____

2. daylight _____

3. diamonds _____

4. ghast _____

5. saddle _____

6. sign _____

What other words with silent letters do you know? Write them here:

1. _____   3. _____

2. _____   4. _____

WITHER'S SIGHT WORD SEARCH

Find the sight words in the puzzle below and circle them.
Hint: Words can be backwards!

all	use	play	has
both	boy	will	are
that	from	the	can
said	look	she	you

```
S A I D E L S G T
P Q T H H N Y H Z
D L T A U W X O E
K T S S H N I Y B
H O E R A T A L Y
V T O Y X L M C L
R J O L P O L L A
L U R B R M J Z D
V N J F X B J N L
```

SIGHT WORD REVIEW

Copy the words on the space provided.

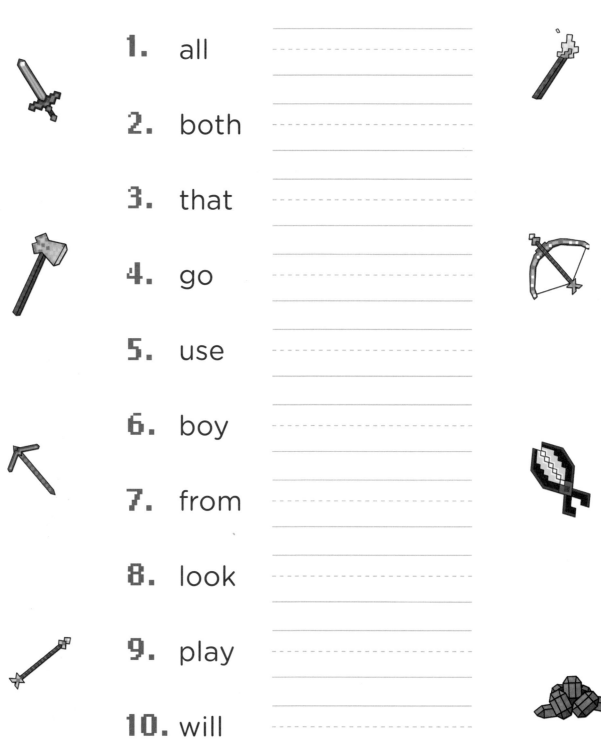

1. all

2. both

3. that

4. go

5. use

6. boy

7. from

8. look

9. play

10. will

SPELLING TEST 1 SIGHT WORDS

*Time to do some wordcrafting! Have a parent or friend read the List 1 words to you **(on page 52)** and see how many you can spell correctly.*

Date: _____

Number correct: _____

1. _____

2. _____

3. _____

4. _____

5. _____

6. _____

7. _____

8. _____

9. _____

10. _____

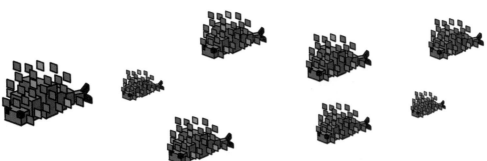

SIGHT WORD REVIEW

Copy the words on the space provided.

1. the

2. she

3. it

4. has

5. are

6. can

7. you

8. we

9. said

10. do

SPELLING TEST 2 SIGHT WORDS

*Time to do some wordcrafting! Have a parent or friend read the List 2 words to you **(on page 54)** and see how many you can spell correctly.*

Date: _____

Number correct: _____

1. _____

2. _____

3. _____

4. _____

5. _____

6. _____

7. _____

8. _____

9. _____

10. _____

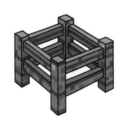

ALPHABETICAL ORDER

Write the words below in alphabetical order on the spaces provided.

shield	block	zombie
dragon	ghast	torch
chest	creeper	blaze
mob	potion	

1. _____

2. _____

3. _____

4. _____

5. _____

6. _____

7. _____

8. _____

9. _____

10. _____

11. _____

MINECRAFTING WORD FIND

Find the Minecrafting words in the puzzle below and circle them. Hint: Words can be backwards!

shield   dragon   chest   mob

block   ghast   creeper   potion

zombie   torch   blaze

C S H I E L D Z W

D R M C Y Z O M L

R G E O R M A N Y

A H Y E B O O L B

G A T I P I T L B

O S E S T E O W M

N T X O E C R T Y

W N P N K H B Q J

W Z R Q N D C Z T

ANSWERS

Page 2, Missing Letter
1) a
2) u
3) i
4) a
5) e

Page 3, Building Words
1) cat
2) hug
3) pig
4) bat
5) egg

Page 4, Sight Word Fill-in
1) walk
2) her
3) how
4) some, and
5) over

Page 5, Sight Word Scramble
1) over
2) how
3) her
4) and
5) some
6) walk

Page 7, Beginnning Sounds
1) b
2) d
3) c
4) m
5) f

Page 8, Punctuation Power
1) Steve is mining for gems.
2) Steve is using his pickaxe to break the block.
3) The block is difficult to break.
4) It is good that Steve is so strong.

Page 9, Missing Letter
1) e
2) u
3) e
4) u
5) e

Page 10, Building Words
1) web
2) sun
3) pen
4) run
5) leg

Page 11, Sight Word Fill-in
1) Both
2) that
3) all
4) use
5) go

Page 12, Sight Word Scramble
1) use
2) both
3) all
4) that
5) go

Page 14, Slime's Rhyme Challenge
1) fun
2) egg
3) Endermen
4) cup
Answers may vary.

Page 15, Word Crafting
Answers may vary. Some answers include: tan, pan, fan, can, lap, flap, pant, pet, pen, net, flat, tune, out, one

Page 16, Missing Letter

1) o
2) i
3) i
4) o
5) o

Page 17 Building Words

1) dog
2) six
3) big
4) mobs
5) hop

Page 18, Sight Word Fill-In

1) boy
2) play
3) look
4) from
5) will

Page 20, Find and Fix

1) play
2) will
3) look
4) from
5) boys

Page 21, Ending Sounds

1) l
2) n
3) d
4) r
5) p

Page 22, Missing Letter

1) blaze
2) bone
3) cave
4) write
5) cube

Page 23, Sight Word Scramble

1) blaze
2) bone
3) write
4) cave
5) five
6) fire or flame

Page 24, Sight Word Fill-In

1) it
2) are
3) the
4) has
5) she

Page 25, Building Words

1) are
2) it
3) the or she
4) has
5) she or the

Page 27, Find and Fix

1) she
2) the
3) has
4) it
5) are

Page 28, Beginning Sound Match-Up

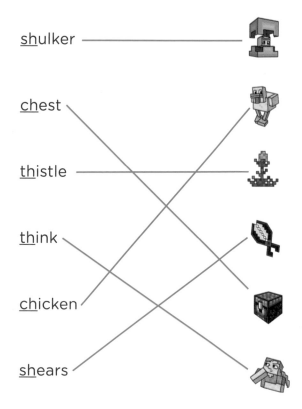

shulker

chest

thistle

think

chicken

shears

Page 29, Ending Sound Match-Up

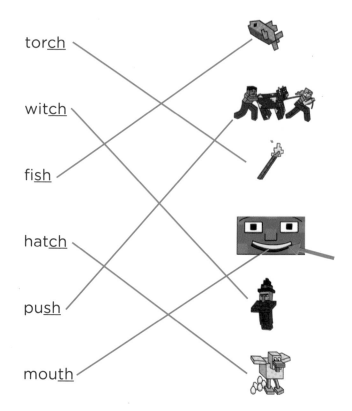

tor<u>ch</u>

wit<u>ch</u>

fi<u>sh</u>

hat<u>ch</u>

pu<u>sh</u>

mou<u>th</u>

Page 30, Long and Short Vowels
1) inventory (short)
2) time (long)
3) ink sac (short)
4) slime (long)
5) villager (short)

Page 31, Long and Short Vowels
1) Enderman (short)
2) tree (long)
3) sheep (long)
4) skeleton (short)
5) beef (long)

Page 32, Long and Short Vowels
1) arrow (long)
2) zombie (short)
3) block (short)
4) glowstone (both are long)
5) potion (long)

Page 33, Long and Short Vowels
1) axe (short)
2) attack (short)
3) cake (long)
4) hat (short)
5) ghast (short)

Page 34, Long and Short Vowels
1) pufferfish (short)
2) cube (long)
3) blue (long)
4) husk (short)
5) drumstick (short)

Page 35, Sight Word Fill-In
1) can
2) said
3) we
4) do
5) you

Page 36, Sight Word Scramble
1) do
2) said
3) can
4) you
5) we

Page 38, Rhyme Time
1. sword
2. slow
3. table
4. potion
5. ladder

Page 39, Count the Syllables
1) 2
2) 2
3) 3
4) 1
5) 3

Page 40, Word Crafting
Answers may vary. Possible answers include: man, sad, red, bin, rib, mob, ran, brain, bone, dim, bird, nod, rob, some, mean, sand

Page 41, Punctuation Power
1. There are many zombies.
2. Zombie pigmen live in the Nether.
3. Zombies attack villagers.
4. Zombies burn in the daylight.
5. They come out at night.

Page 42, Creeper's Capital Letter Quest
1. When Alex saw the ocelot, she ran over to it.
2. Steve gave Alex some fish so she could tame it.
3. The ocelot ate Alex's fish and turned into a cat.
4. Alex named her pet cat Savannah.
5. Savannah scared away all the creepers.

Page 43, Find and Fix
1. do
2. said
3. can
4. we
5. You

Page 44, Vowel Teams
1. h
2. a
3. r
4. t
5. e
6. t
7. ee and ea

Page 45, Vowel Teams

1. r
2. b
3. n
4. o
5. b
6. o
7. ee and oo

Page 46, Slime's Rhyme Challenge

1) Grass   Glass   ☑
2) Enderman   Endermite   ☐
3) Slime   Time   ☑
4) Craft   Blast   ☐
5) Teeth   Wheat   ☐
6) Armor   Farmer   ☑

Page 47, Beginning Blends

1) dragon   dr
2) Steve   St
3) blaze   bl
4) spider   sp
5) snow golem   sn
6) squid   sq

Page 48, Ending Blends

1. wing   ng
2. firework   rk
3. sword   rd
4. ghast   st
5. shield   ld
6. chest   st

Page 49, Count the Syllables

1. 4
2. 2
3. 3
4. 3
5. 1

Page 50, Find the Silent Letter

1. w
2. g
3. a
4. h
5. e
6. g
Answers may vary.

Page 51, Wither's Sight Word Search

Page 56, Alphabetical Order

blaze
block
chest
creeper
dragon
ghast
shield
torch
zombie

Page 57, Minecrafting Word Find

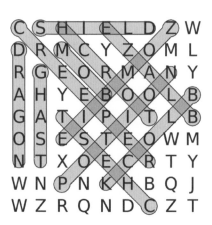